CW01512593

Original title:
Hazel Shards Beneath the Elf Cusp

Author: Swan Charm
ISBN HARDBACK: 978-1-80563-120-0
ISBN PAPERBACK: 978-1-80564-641-9

Ethereal Echoes in the Fae Grove

In the grove where whispers flow,
Shadows dance, and breezes blow.
Glimmers twinkle, soft and bright,
Calling softly through the night.

Beneath the leaves, the secrets sing,
Echoes of an ancient spring.
Fairy lights in the twilight haze,
Guide the lost in mystic ways.

Moonlit paths of emerald green,
Where unseen creatures have been.
A laughter woven into air,
Promises made in the twilight's glare.

In every nook, a tale is spun,
Of battles fought and glories won.
The echoing haunts of ancient lore,
Lead us to the enchanted door.

So linger long where faeries tread,
In the dreams that weave through thread.
A world alive with gentle sighs,
In the grove where wonder lies.

Shimmering Bits of Hidden Magic

In every corner, glistens light,
Whispers weave through the day and night.
A sprinkle of stardust, small and bright,
Hints at tales of wonder in flight.

Petals dance on the morning dew,
Secrets held in every hue.
A glimmer catches the eye's delight,
Magic lurks just out of sight.

With every breeze, the stories flow,
Ancient spells that ebb and glow.
Each rustle hints of things unseen,
In the spaces where we dream.

In shadows deep, the mysteries play,
A flicker beckons; shall we stay?
To chase the sparks that weave and spin,
In the magic that dwells within.

So gather 'round, let imagination soar,
In hidden realms of ancient lore.
For every shimmer holds a key,
To unlock the world's sweet fantasy.

Secrets of the Verdant Veil

Beyond the thicket, paths unwind,
Where untold wonders we may find.
Secrets buried beneath the vine,
Whisper softly, 'All will be fine.'

The canopy drapes in layers green,
Hiding sights that have ne'er been seen.
In every shadow, stories bloom,
Of spirits dwelling in the gloom.

With footsteps light, we tread the earth,
Where each seed holds a tale of birth.
The murmurs of leaves, a symphony,
Drawing us deeper into harmony.

From hidden glades, where echoes call,
Adventure waits, just past the wall.
In luminous mist, we shall unveil,
The secrets wrapped in the verdant veil.

So let us roam through this enchanted wood,
Where dreams awaken, as they should.
The magic whispers, drawing near,
In the heart of nature, free from fear.

Luminous Splinters of Arcane Dreams

In twilight's grasp, the visions bloom,
Underneath the stars' gentle loom.
Each splintered light, a tale to weave,
Of grand adventures, believe!

Through tangled stars, the dreams cascade,
A tapestry of night is made.
Shimmering fragments touch the soul,
Leading hearts to their greater goal.

The air hums with arcane tunes,
Dancing bright as the silver moons.
From every glimmer, magic flows,
In whispers soft, the wonder grows.

So linger here and let it rise,
Within the depths, where freedom lies.
Each luminous spark, a path we take,
Into worlds where no one wakes.

Embrace the night, let dreams ignite,
With every breath, a new delight.
For in these splinters, truths be told,
In arcane realms, our fate unfolds.

Interludes from the Fairywood

In twilight's grace, the shadows play,
With whispers soft, they weave the day.
Amidst the trees, a secret song,
Where fairies dance, the night feels long.

Moonbeams sprinkle upon the glade,
Awakening dreams that never fade.
The breeze carries tales on silver wings,
Of ancient lore and wondrous things.

Each flower glows with a whispered charm,
While starlight wraps the world in calm.
The heart of wood, alive with light,
A symphony of magic, pure delight.

In every nook, a tale is spun,
Of love and laughter, lost and won.
Through rustling leaves, the stories swirl,
In Fairywood, let dreams unfurl.

Glowing Pellets of Celestial Wonder

In midnight skies, where stardust falls,
Glimmers of hope in silence calls.
Small glowing pellets light the way,
Guiding the lost at end of day.

They dance on winds, so light and free,
A glimpse of what we're meant to see.
With every flicker, hearts ignite,
In celestial realms, pure and bright.

Wrapped in shadows, they brightly gleam,
Whispers of promises in a dream.
Each tiny orb, a wish set free,
Echoes of sorrows, sweet jubilee.

Journey onward, through cosmic tide,
In glowing light, let hope abide.
For in the dark, these wonders sing,
A melody of light, the night can bring.

Mirrored Secrets of the Nature's Commune

Reflections dance on crystal streams,
Mirrored secrets hide in dreams.
The forest breathes a tale untold,
In every leaf, a memory old.

Beneath the boughs, whispers unite,
Nature's heart, a guide through night.
With every rustle, a truth revealed,
In sacred woods, our fate is sealed.

Across the glen, where shadows wane,
The earth reveals both joy and pain.
In every branch that sways and bends,
The spirit of nature gently mends.

In rustling winds, the stories cry,
Of life and loss, we learn to fly.
Through mirrored paths both dark and light,
We find our way, igniting the night.

Shards of Magic in the Leafy Depths

Hidden deep where sunlight fades,
Shards of magic weave through glades.
In leafy depths, enchantments lie,
Waiting for souls who seek the sky.

Crimson petals and emerald vines,
Hold the secrets of ancient signs.
With every step, the silence hums,
As nature's breath in whispers comes.

Fingers brush 'gainst velvet moss,
In the quiet, we embrace the loss.
Yet in the shadows, wonders bloom,
Rich with magic, dispelling gloom.

The heart of the forest, alive and wise,
Invites the dreamer to realize.
Through every shard, a story waits,
Of hopes and fears, our tangled fates.

Amongst the Woven Shadows of the Night

In shadows deep where whispers dwell,
The moonlight weaves a silver spell.
Creatures dance in the cool, dark air,
Secrets shimmer, beyond compare.

A flicker here, a glance from there,
Ebon wings that softly flare.
Hearts entwined in a silent call,
Evening's magic enfolds us all.

Dreams woven from starlit threads,
Carry hopes where night gently treads.
Through twisting paths of ancient trees,
Daring souls find the fabled keys.

In hidden realms where time stands still,
Mysterious tales our hearts fulfill.
Listen closely, the night reveals,
All the wonders a shadow conceals.

So linger long in this hushed retreat,
Let moonlit magic guide your feet.
Amongst the woven shadows bright,
Find yourself in the heart of night.

Flickers of Soul in the Faerie Glade

Amidst the boughs where fairies play,
Soft laughter echoes, come what may.
Petal whispers, a gentle tune,
Twilight dances beneath the moon.

Glimmers bright in emerald light,
Lost in dreams both sweet and slight.
Hand in hand, with spirits free,
We sway to the faerie's melody.

Beneath the trees where secrets bloom,
Time hurries forth in soft perfume.
Each flicker holds a tale untold,
Of hearts entwined, both brave and bold.

In circles drawn with beams of gold,
Magic gathers, a sight to behold.
Weaving wishes through misty air,
In this glade, no worries to bear.

So linger here, where dreams unite,
Feel the warmth of a faerie's light.
In this enchanted, sacred space,
Flickers of soul find their place.

Sprites' Secrets in Silvery Haze

In dawn's embrace, the spirits play,
Sprites take wing at break of day.
Whispers soft in the morning dew,
Secrets shine in their playful hue.

A silver haze cloaks the bright morn,
Stirring magic, anew and reborn.
Through fields aglow with wild delight,
Mischief twinkles in gentle light.

A hidden laugh, a sweet refrain,
Echoing joys like softly falling rain.
Every rustle tells a story rare,
In sylvan woods, with secrets to share.

Glimmering trails where fairies roam,
Inviting souls to find their home.
With every flutter, hearts align,
In the hush of dawn, their spirits shine.

So follow the path where sprites cascade,
In the silvery haze, dreams are made.
Unravel the tales held dear and close,
In the heart of wonder, where magic flows.

Gems of Dawn Hidden in the Thicket

Amidst the thicket where shadows play,
Gems of dawn chase the night away.
Crimson hues in a gentle rise,
A tapestry spun across the skies.

With every breath, the world awakes,
In whispered hues, the silence breaks.
Nature's canvas, brushed with grace,
In morning's light, our hearts find place.

Petals unfurl, a sight to behold,
In dew-kissed glades, stories unfold.
Each gem aglow with dreams anew,
Awakening spirits, bold and true.

When day breaks forth, a soft embrace,
The thicket glows, a sacred space.
We venture forth, hand in hand,
To cherish the beauty of this land.

So seek the gems where dawn does gleam,
In the thicket's heart, follow the dream.
Here in the light, our spirits soar,
Hidden treasures forevermore.

Charmed Nuggets of the Forest Floor

Beneath the boughs of ancient trees,
Nuggets gleam in whispered breeze.
Tiny treasures rest in green,
Where magic weaves through every scene.

Mossy carpets hide their glow,
Secrets wait for hearts to know.
Each pebble sings of tales untold,
In nature's arms, the wonders unfold.

Twilight dances, shadows play,
Softly urging night to sway.
With every step on soft earth's bed,
Dreams awaken, secrets spread.

Crickets serenade the dusk,
In the air, a gentle musk.
Flickering fireflies, lanterns bright,
Guide the way through the quiet night.

Charmed nuggets, lost and found,
In the symphony of sound.
Fables linger where we roam,
In the heart of this enchanted home.

Enigmatic Twinkles Amongst the Leaves

Amidst the shadows of the wood,
Twinkles dance where dreams once stood.
Beams of light in emerald lace,
Call to wanderers to embrace.

Whispers weave through leafy veins,
Echoing in gentle refrains.
Each heartbeat thrives in nature's song,
In this world where all belong.

Laughter floats on fragrant air,
As magic swirls without a care.
The mystery of the night unfolds,
In every glimmer, a story told.

Beneath the stars, the forest sighs,
With every twinkle, the spirit flies.
Enchantments linger, soft and sweet,
In twilight's arms, the soul's retreat.

A gathering of sparkles bright,
Nestled softly in the night.
Find your heart where shadows weave,
Amongst the leaves, dare to believe.

Glinting Memories of Sylvan Lore

In the woods where legends dwell,
Glinting memories softly swell.
Each branch and bough a keeper's tome,
Preserving whispers of our home.

Footfalls echo on the glade,
Stories swaying with each cascade.
Colors splash where sunlight plays,
In the shade, old magic stays.

Time slips through the gentle trees,
Carried forth on a playful breeze.
Minds awaken with the dawn,
To stir the dreams that linger on.

Fables etched in bark and stone,
Sublime enchantments softly sewn.
The sylvan tales breathe life anew,
Guiding hearts in every hue.

Glinting memories, lost in time,
Whispering rhymes in rhythmic chime.
Awaken, wanderers, take flight,
For lore awaits beyond the night.

Fragments of a Dreamy Whimsy

In a world of bright, soft dreams,
Whimsy dances, playful themes.
Gossamer threads of thought take wing,
In each moment, joy we bring.

Petals flutter on the breeze,
Tickled whispers through the trees.
Dew-kissed mornings, sparkling bright,
Encourage hearts to take new flight.

Echoes of laughter fill the air,
Fragrant blooms beyond compare.
Imagination strides along,
In the heart where dreams belong.

Wander through this magical maze,
Let your spirit join the praise.
For in each step, a tale ignites,
And laughter shares the starlit nights.

Fragments scatter, soft as light,
In the canvas of the night.
Capture whimsy, hold it near,
For every moment, crystal clear.

Light's Tapestry among the Fir Trees

In the stillness of the night,
Stars weave stories in the sky.
Fir trees stand, their branches dance,
With whispers of the moon's soft sigh.

Golden beams through needles stray,
Casting patterns on the floor.
Squirrels scurry, night at play,
As fireflies blink, a magic chore.

Glimmers weave through tangled boughs,
Nature's quilt, a subtle thread.
Breath of pine, the forest vows,
In whispers of the paths we tread.

Hope ignites where shadows blend,
A spark of light in darkened glen.
Where secrets linger, dreams ascends,
Among the firs, we find our zen.

Luminous trails that lead us on,
Through the realm of ancient trees.
The tapestry of dusk will dawn,
And guide our hearts with gentle ease.

Glistening Hopes in Woodland Shadows

Amidst the leaves, the sunlight plays,
A glimmer sparkles, soft and bright.
Through tangled roots, in dim delays,
Hopes shimmer, whispering of light.

The brook sings sweet beneath the trees,
Its laughter mingles with the breeze.
Each note a promise, soft and clear,
Glistening hopes, the heart shall steer.

Veils of mist in twilight's fold,
Hide the magic yet to unfold.
With every step on mossy ground,
The joy of life through trees is found.

Crickets chirp their evening song,
While shadows deepen, day is gone.
In every pause, where dreams belong,
Hope's glistening thread will linger on.

With every path, uncertainty,
Yet glistening dreams in shadows call.
We dance where nature's laughter be,
And find our strength where fears fall small.

Where Echoes Whisper in the Underbrush

In tangled hues of green and brown,
Echoes linger in the air.
Tiny creatures scurry round,
While secrets roam without a care.

Softly rustling leaves impart,
Stories hidden in their weave.
Whispers bounce from heart to heart,
In this realm, we dare believe.

Each footstep stirs the quiet ground,
Awakening the slumbered lore.
Ancient tales in silence drown,
Yet in the underbrush, they soar.

Where echoes speak, and shadows sway,
A symphony of life and grace.
In nature's arms, we lose our way,
And find the magic in the space.

From ferns that bow to creatures rare,
To beams of light that guide us through,
Each echo holds a secret prayer,
That whispers hope and life anew.

Fables of the Forest's Hidden Heart

In forest deep, where fables bloom,
Whispers twine with every breeze.
The heart of woods holds tales of doom,
And dreams that dance among the trees.

Where shadows gather, stories grow,
Of elves and beasts, both shy and bold.
With every leaf that falls, we know,
The legends cherished, never old.

Dappled light on paths untraveled,
Calls forth the brave to seek their fate.
In every tale, a truth unraveled,
A journey waiting, never late.

The hidden heart beats soft and strong,
A rhythm felt beneath the ground.
In every branch, a haunting song,
Of lovers lost and hope profound.

So pause a while, and listen dear,
Let rustling leaves your heart embrace.
For fables here bring joy and fear,
In the forest's warm and wild grace.

Sighs Beneath the Ancient Bough

Whispers linger in the air,
Underneath the ancient tree,
Secrets held in branches bare,
Guarded by the roots so free.

Sighs of ages softly weave,
Tales of magic, love, and pain,
In the twilight, hearts believe,
In the solace of the rain.

Gnarled fingers stretch for sky,
Each leaf speaks of times gone by,
Mossy blankets on the ground,
In this stillness, peace is found.

Shadows dance with fading light,
Nature whispers, drawing near,
Underneath the velvet night,
All our worries disappear.

Dreams take flight on twilight wings,
Carried by the evening breeze,
As the night with magic sings,
In the heart of ancient trees.

The Melodies of the Forest's Soul

Amidst the trees, a song is spun,
With rustling leaves, the day is done,
A choir of crickets, nightingale,
In harmony, they weave a tale.

Raindrops tap on branches high,
Nature hums a lullaby,
Every note, a gentle sigh,
Echoing through the moonlit sky.

Beneath the stars, the forest dreams,
Of silver streams and sunlit beams,
Melodies of shadows play,
Guiding wanderers on their way.

The wind carries secrets wide,
Through the trees where spirits bide,
Echo of a whispered name,
In this place, we'll never be the same.

In the depths where wild hearts roam,
The forest calls us all to home,
With every pulse, every beat,
The soul of nature, pure and sweet.

Enchanted Textures of the Verdant Realm

The emerald hues of whispered green,
Wrap the world in velvet sheen,
Every petal, every vine,
Speaks of magic, old designs.

Fuzzy moss beneath my feet,
Where ferns and blooming wonders meet,
Textures rich, a soft embrace,
Nature's art, a sacred space.

Sunlight dapples through the leaves,
Crafting shadows where one believes,
Every bark and textured trail,
Tells a story, sweet and frail.

A tapestry of life in bloom,
Filling every inch of room,
Insects hum a gentle tune,
Underneath the silver moon.

In each corner, beauty lies,
Where the heart soars and grief flies,
In the realm where dreams unfurl,
Enchanted textures shape our world.

The Sundown's Embrace in Nature's Lap

As daylight bids the world adieu,
A canvas painted gold and blue,
The sun dips low beyond the hills,
Nature wraps its heart in thrills.

Crickets chirp, the stars ignite,
Arraying jewels in the night,
The warm embrace of dusk unfolds,
With whispered tales of love untold.

Tree shadows gradually stretch long,
Swaying gently to the song,
Of twilight breezes, soft and sweet,
In nature's lap, our hearts do meet.

Fireflies dance in glowing light,
Memories spark in the fading night,
Each flicker a wish to hold,
In the magic, brave and bold.

As day transforms to gentle dark,
The whispers shift, and life embarks,
In nature's arms, we come to rest,
In the sundown's embrace, we're blessed.

Ethereal Glimmers among the Leaves

In the dappled light of day,
Glimmers weave through the trees,
Whispers soft as the twilight,
Fluttering on the gentle breeze.

A dance of shadows and whispers,
Secrets tucked in the boughs,
Fairy lights spark in the dusk,
Nature's magic, here and now.

Ferns unfurl like stories told,
The past cradled in their fronds,
Muffled laughter of the sprites,
Echoes woven in the ponds.

Golden rays paint the forest,
In hues of amber and green,
Every glint a fleeting moment,
A glimpse of what once had been.

Beneath the canopy so wide,
Dreams flutter like summer wings,
In the hush of the woodland heart,
The symphony of nature sings.

Secrets of the Sylvan Grove

In the shade of ancient oaks,
Whispers play upon the breeze,
Gnarled roots hold tales of old,
Carved in knots, beneath the leaves.

Moonlight dances on the brook,
Casting charms on stones aglow,
Linden scents the balmy night,
Protecting all with secrets low.

Hushed are the thoughts of wanderers,
As they tread on forest floor,
Finding solace in the quiet,
Discovering all that came before.

Sylvan spirits gleam and twirl,
With every rustle of the bark,
A ballet of soft shadows,
Charmed by whispers in the dark.

Amidst the ferns, the echoes play,
Inviting hearts to pause and see,
The grove is a book of wonders,
Revealing life's sweet mystery.

Dance of the Sunlit Petals

Blossoms greet the morning sun,
Dancing with the gentle light,
Colors splash across the glade,
A festival in bloom so bright.

Honeybees hum in delight,
Flitting from bloom to bloom,
Nature's symphony of life,
Filling the air with sweet perfume.

Fluttering in a playful breeze,
Petals swirl like dreams unbound,
Every hue tells a story,
In the dance where joy is found.

Golden rays guide the way,
Through gardens lush and fair,
Each blossom a note in harmony,
Painting beauty everywhere.

And as the day starts to wane,
Petals close in soft repose,
Whispers of the twilight air,
Guarding secrets that nature chose.

Echoes of Enchantment in the Forest

In the heart of the whispering woods,
A melody lingers near,
Echoes dance through the silence,
Carried on wings of cheer.

Moonlit paths invite the bold,
To wander and weave through night,
Each step a note, a story told,
By starlit whispers, soft and light.

Misty tendrils curl like dreams,
Embracing the night's embrace,
Every shadow holds a tale,
In this enchanted, secret place.

Crickets serenade the dark,
With songs of love and lore,
While fireflies paint the air,
With magic folklore to explore.

As dawn peeks through the trees,
The echoes fade with the night,
Yet the forest keeps its secrets,
In the beauty of morning light.

Sylphs and the Glittering Remnants

In twilight's hush, they start to dance,
With whispers soft, they weave their chance.
Through ancient woods, on silver beams,
They flit and float like wandering dreams.

Their laughter twirls in evening's glow,
Among the blooms where secrets flow.
With gossamer wings, in playful flight,
They chase the dusk and beckon night.

In moonlit glades, where shadows play,
They gather stardust, bright and gay.
Each twinkle sings of realms unknown,
Where magic stirs and hearts are thrown.

With whispered tales of times gone by,
They lead the lost to realms on high.
In silver streams, their stories gleam,
A world awake, alive with dream.

So heed the call in twilight's realm,
Where sylphs and secrets at dusk overwhelm.
Their glittering remnants softly fade,
In hearts anew, their magic laid.

Nature's Glistening Tales Untold

Amidst the trees, where shadows blend,
Nature whispers, her stories mend.
With every leaf, a tale unfolds,
Of whispered secrets and truths of old.

The brook babbles with a gentle sound,
As sunlight filters through the ground.
In every ripple, history flows,
A timeless dance that only grows.

The breeze carries tales of the past,
Of fleeting moments that never last.
In blooming flowers, legends bloom,
Fragrant whispers dispel the gloom.

The mountain stands, its tale profound,
With each stone laid, a story bound.
From deep within, its spirit sighs,
In echoes soft, where creation lies.

So listen close to nature's heart,
For every end brings forth a start.
In glistening tales, both wild and free,
Lies the magic of what's yet to be.

Radiance of the Eldritch Woods

In Eldritch Woods, where shadows weave,
A tapestry of dreams they'll leave.
The ancient trees stand tall and wise,
Guardians of secrets beneath the skies.

Their branches sway with a gentle grace,
An invitation to a hidden place.
Where faeries hide in the dappled light,
And dusk brings forth the dance of night.

The air is thick with magic's song,
A melody where spirits throng.
In every glimmer, a whisper shared,
Of gentle hearts who've always cared.

The moonlight bathes the forest floor,
As shadows flicker, and spirits soar.
With every step, the ground provides,
A path where wonder ever abides.

So venture forth, with heart held high,
Through Eldritch Woods where dreams can fly.
For in this realm, both wild and grand,
Radiance glows from every strand.

Threads of Twinkling Enchantment

In twilight's embrace, we soon shall find,
Threads of enchantment, woven and twined.
With each gentle breeze, a story spins,
Of hope and magic that quietly wins.

The stars above, like crystals bright,
Guide our dreams through the cloak of night.
In every shimmer, a wish takes flight,
Painting the heavens in joyous light.

The winding paths where willows weep,
Hold secrets buried, both wide and deep.
With every whisper of rustling leaves,
A promise unfolds, as twilight weaves.

The moonlight kisses the emerald glen,
A moment captured, again and again.
With threads of silver, the night begins,
A symphony sung by twilight's kin.

So let your heart be open wide,
To the magic that flows like a timeless tide.
With every thread, a tale ignites,
Of twinkling enchantment in starry nights.

Intricate Whispers of the Woodlands

In the glade where shadows play,
Whispers weave through dusk's soft breath,
Branches bend in gentle sway,
Carrying tales of life and death.

Mossy carpets cradle feet,
Where secrets fade into the mist,
Every rustle, every beat,
Hints of magic, softly kissed.

Elder trees stand tall and wise,
Their bark adorned with stories old,
In their gaze, the past still lies,
A tapestry of dreams retold.

Moonlight spills like silver threads,
Dancing softly on the brook,
In this realm where silence treads,
Every glance, a hidden nook.

So wander here, where whispers cling,
To heartbeats hidden out of sight,
In the woodland's sacred ring,
Find the magic, pure delight.

Whispers of the Woodland Veil

Beyond the thicket, stories sigh,
Amidst the ferns and tender leaves,
Where shadows dance and echoes lie,
The woodland veil softly weaves.

Crickets sing a twilight tune,
Stars awaken in the haze,
Gentle breezes lift the gloom,
As night slips in and day decays.

Glimmers peek through branches bare,
Nature's whispers, sweet and light,
In every heartbeat, every stare,
Mysteries wrapped in starlit night.

Underneath the ancient trees,
Lost dreams linger with the dew,
Their secrets carried on the breeze,
Softly singing, ever true.

So listen close, for tales await,
In whispers woven, soft and bright,
The woodland bears a timeless fate,
Of magic spun in night's delight.

Elven Lament in Twilight's Glow

Beneath the twilight's silver sheen,
Elven hearts entwined in woe,
Forests cradle what's unseen,
In shadows where the lost dreams go.

Softly hum the leaves above,
Whispers linger on the air,
A haunting song of bygone love,
Of paths once walked, yet now so rare.

Glistening tears like morning dew,
Fall upon the earth's embrace,
In every sigh, a tale rings true,
Of fleeting time, a gentle trace.

The stars in sorrow seem to weep,
For moments lost to endless night,
Yet linger still, through shadows deep,
In twilight's glow, a flickering light.

So take heed of elven grace,
For all that's lost shall find its way,
In every heart and secret space,
Love endures, though skies turn gray.

Fragments of Autumn's Embrace

In autumn's tender, golden light,
Leaves decay with whispered grace,
Each fragment drifts on gentle flight,
A dance of time in nature's space.

Crisp air carries scents of change,
Burnished hues adorn the trees,
World transformed, a canvas strange,
Where silence hums a melody.

Underneath the harvest moon,
Beneath a quilt of twilight's thread,
Hope embers in the cooling tune,
As summer's warmth slips on ahead.

With every rustle, echoes near,
A tapestry of loss and gain,
In each soft breath, the end draws near,
Yet promises of spring remain.

So cherish now the fleeting glow,
In fragments, beauty finds its mark,
For autumn's love, in soft winds blow,
A whispered hope, a tender spark.

Fleeting Whispers of the Old Oak

In the heart of the forest, a giant stands tall,
With branches that cradle the twilight's soft call.
Its leaves catch the secrets of ages gone by,
Whispered tales of the kingdom beneath the wide sky.

Beneath its great boughs, the shadows entwine,
A tapestry woven with old magic divine.
The roots stretch like fingers through earth rich and deep,
Guarding the stories that nature must keep.

When the twilight approaches, its wisdom takes flight,
Guiding the lost through the cloak of the night.
For every faint sigh of the breeze that may pass,
Tales of the ancients weave soft on the grass.

With each passing season, new whispers arise,
Of dreams that once blossomed, now lost to the skies.
Yet through all the ages, the oak will remain,
A guardian of wonders, through joy and through pain.

So pause for a moment, beneath its grand shade,
And listen for echoes of magic displayed.
For in fleeting whispers, the old oak does share,
The timeless connection that binds us all there.

Glimmers of Magic in the Mist

As dawn paints the world with a soft, gentle hue,
Mists weave their magic, revealing the new.
The air shimmers brightly, alive with a spark,
Where dreams blend with reality, in twilight's sweet arc.

Tread lightly through whispers that dance in the light,
For shadows play tricks as day turns to night.
A flicker of starlight hangs low on a leaf,
A moment of wonder, both poignant and brief.

The forest awakens, the creatures take flight,
With glimmers of magic that punctuate night.
Faint echoes of laughter weave through the trees,
As faeries wrap sparkles in soft autumn's breeze.

In this realm of enchantment where time seems to pause,
The heart hears the rhythm of nature's applause.
So linger a while, let your spirit be free,
As glimmers of magic entwine you with me.

For each drop of dew is a pearl from the sky,
A testament glowing that haste must deny.
In the dance of the mist, embrace the unknown,
For magic surrounds us, where'er we have flown.

Petals of Light on a Dusky Path

When twilight descends and the stars start to gleam,
A winding path beckons, like threads of a dream.
Petals of light fall where shadows can blend,
Carrying whispers of journeys to mend.

Through thickets of silence, with courage in stride,
Each step on this journey swells hope deep inside.
The night wraps in velvet, the world softly sighs,
While moonbeams cascade like soft lullabies.

With pockets of starlight, the lanterns ignite,
Illuminating shadows that dance with delight.
For every heart wanders, each spirit alights,
In the glow of the petals, their wishes take flight.

The fables of ferns and the tales of the night,
Whisper of magic in every soft light.
With every petal casting a glow, pure and bright,
The dusky path leads us to dreams out of sight.

So follow the trail where the petal dust sways,
With each step unfolding the wonders of days.
For the journey itself is both thick and profound,
In the heart of the dusk, let your true self be found.

The Enchanted Stream's Serenade

Where the water does whisper and softly does flow,
The stream weaves a story, both gentle and slow.
With glimmers of starlight reflecting on waves,
It serenades nature, with secrets it saves.

Through banks lush and vibrant, the willows will sway,
As time softly dances in languid ballet.
The melody swirls in the cool evening air,
A soothe to the heart, like a lover's sweet care.

Its ripples reveal what the eyes cannot see,
A world of enchantment, where spirits roam free.
Each stone tells a story, each eddy a song,
With echoes of magic that linger so long.

As twilight embraces the stream's gentle heart,
Each twinkle of water becomes its own art.
In caresses of light, let the worries disperse,
For the serenade lingers, a spell to immerse.

So wander beside it, while twilight extends,
Feel the pulse of the stream, where the journey transcends.

In the whispers of waters and soft moon-kissed beams,
Find solace and hope in the fabric of dreams.

Memories of Lost Elves among the Pines

In shadows deep where whispers dwell,
The echoes of the past do tell,
Of elves who danced in twilight's glow,
Now bound to earth, where no winds blow.

Their laughter rings through boughs so high,
A fleeting song that bids goodbye.
The pines they loved, in silence weep,
Guarding secrets they shall keep.

Once shimmering in starlit skies,
Their spirits drift like fireflies.
Each twinkle fades, a tearful sigh,
They fade away, yet never die.

Among the trees, their shadows play,
In memory's arms, they gently stay.
The forest holds their tales so dear,
In every rustle, they are near.

So venture forth, and heed the call,
For in the pines, they still enthrall.
With every step, the magic swells,
Among the lost, the laughter dwells.

The Celestial Glimmers of the Glade

In the heart of the glade, where starlight gleams,
A tapestry woven of silver dreams.
Each glimmer whispers a tale untold,
Of midnight dances and secrets bold.

Beneath the boughs, the shadows play,
While fireflies twinkle to light the way.
The moonlight drapes like a silken sheet,
Where earthly souls and stardust meet.

The echoes of laughter fill the air,
As if the wind carries a secret affair.
From ancient trees to the soft moss bed,
The stories of ages linger ahead.

With every breeze, the magic swirls,
In the glimmers, the hidden world unfurls.
A place of wonder, hope, and grace,
In the heart of the woods, a sacred space.

So come and wander, let your spirit glide,
In the celestial glade, let dreams reside.
For every glimmer, a promise to share,
Of light and love, forever rare.

Enchantment Nestled in Leafy Nooks

In leafy nooks where shadows dwell,
A whisper of magic weaves its spell.
Each rustling leaf, a serenade,
Of nested dreams in sunlit shade.

Amidst the greens, an elf's delight,
With silver wings that catch the light.
They dance in circles, pure joy they weave,
In the heart of enchantment, they believe.

The flowers blush, their colors bright,
As playful breezes twirl in flight.
In every nook, where secrets hide,
The pulse of nature will not bide.

A symphony stirs in the air so sweet,
As woodland creatures gather to greet.
Their curious eyes, like twinkling stars,
Know well the magic that's truly ours.

So take a breath and close your eyes,
In leafy nooks, where the heart complies.
Embrace the moments, the dreams they bring,
For in nature's arms, our spirits sing.

The Wisp of Dreams in Woodland Air

In the woodland air, where fancies roam,
A wisp of dreams finds its way home.
Carried by whispers, soft as the night,
It dances among the stars' soft light.

With every breeze, a story spins,
Of hidden glades where wonder begins.
The moonbeams filter through branches wide,
As secrets of ages begin to bide.

Glimmers of hope in the twilight glow,
As shadows of magic begin to flow.
The nightingale sings a lullaby sweet,
To cradle the dreams in a rhythmic beat.

With every flutter of wings above,
The woodland hums with joy and love.
In the heart of the night, where spirits play,
The wisp of dreams lights the way.

So hush your thoughts and listen near,
For the whispers of dreams, you shall hear.
In the woodland air, your heart shall dare,
To chase the wisps that wander there.

Threads of Gold in the Enchanted Wood

In twilight's glow, the whispers weave,
Threads of gold, a tale to believe.
Through branches bent with secrets old,
In dancing light, the magic unfolds.

Each step reveals a hidden spark,
Where shadows play and creatures hark.
The fae emerge with laughter bright,
Their wings aglow in fading light.

A brook sings soft with ancient lore,
As leaves entwine, and spirits soar.
In every glade, a story waits,
Of love and dreams, of cherished fates.

With every turn, enchantments call,
In this wood where wonders sprawl.
For here, amidst the emerald shade,
The threads of gold are freely laid.

So wanderer, with heart so bold,
Step lightly on this path of gold.
Embrace the magic, let it flow,
For in this wood, your soul will grow.

Dusk's Silken Veil of Secrets

As dusk descends, a veil is spun,
With whispers soft, the night begun.
The stars embrace the moon's pale beam,
In shadows deep, we weave a dream.

Secrets linger in the twilight air,
A haunting song, a whispered prayer.
With every breeze, a tale is told,
Of lost desires and hearts of gold.

Glimmers dance on the river's edge,
Where reeds murmur from their hedge.
Each note calls forth forgotten years,
Dancing gently through laughter and tears.

The old oak stands, a sentinel wise,
Guarding stories beneath the skies.
In every bough, a mystery stirs,
As night unveils what daylight blurs.

So linger here, amidst the sighs,
Where the moonlight paints the darkened skies.
In this woven dusk, take a chance,
For secrets bloom in twilight's dance.

Reflections in the Forest's Heart

In the forest's heart, where silence breathes,
Reflections dance among the leaves.
A mirrored pool, so deep and clear,
Holds secrets whispered, always near.

The ancient trees, a wisdom profound,
Their gnarled branches cast around.
With every ripple, memories strain,
Time intertwines with joy and pain.

Upon the shore, the ferns unfurl,
As wisps of mist begin to swirl.
Each glance reveals a life once lived,
In the heart of the wood, a tale is hid.

Here, whispers of the past remain,
In gentle breezes, in soft, sweet rain.
The forest breathes, a living art,
In every shade, it plays its part.

So wander 'neath the emerald hue,
And find the dreams once lost to you.
For in the forest's heart, you'll see,
Reflections of your spirit free.

The Dance of the Moonlit Ferns

Beneath the moon, the ferns do sway,
In rhythms soft, in shades of gray.
Their dance ignites the night's embrace,
A tranquil place, a sacred space.

As silver beams cascade like silk,
The world transformed, as smooth as milk.
With every glance, a secret told,
Of magic spun in threads of gold.

The nightingale sings a lullaby,
As stars twinkle in the velvet sky.
Each note a prayer, a wish refined,
In harmony with hearts entwined.

The shadows join in gentle play,
While whispers of the night hold sway.
In every step, the ferns proclaim,
A dance of joy, a sweet refrain.

So come and join this midnight ball,
Where moonlit ferns invite us all.
In nature's grace, we twirl and spin,
The dance of life, where dreams begin.

Where Shadows Dance on Autumn Leaves

In twilight's glow, where whispers creep,
The autumn leaves in silence weep.
Beneath the trees, where shadows play,
The dreams of yore weave through the day.

A rustling breeze, a fleeting sigh,
A secret pact beneath the sky.
With every step, the past awakes,
In every corner, magic shakes.

The golden hues, they fade to gray,
As twilight beckons, shadows sway.
Time weaves a tale, both sweet and deep,
Beneath the boughs, where memories keep.

Each footfall stirs the forest's heart,
A symphony of life to impart.
The echoes of laughter, lost but near,
In autumn's grasp, we hold them dear.

So tread with care on this charmed ground,
For magic lingers all around.
Where shadows dance and secrets weave,
In autumn's grasp, we learn to believe.

The Riddle of the Enchanted Thicket

In a thicket dense, where wonders bloom,
A riddle lies in twilight's gloom.
The leaves, they rustle with ancient lore,
Whispering secrets of times before.

A flicker of light, a shadow's grin,
Hints at the magic that dwells within.
Paths twist and turn like a pondering thought,
Lost in the maze where tales are brought.

The rustling branches, the soft, cool sigh,
Call to the dreamers who wander nigh.
With every step, the heart beats fast,
As riddles unfold from the shadows cast.

Listen closely to the night's soft tone,
For wisdom dwells in silence grown.
A flickering glow at the thicket's end,
Awaiting the soul who dares to mend.

So venture forth, let curiosity reign,
In the enchanted thicket, break every chain.
For only the brave will choose to find,
The riddle woven in the whispers blind.

Voices of Ancients in the Canopy

In the canopy high, where silence reigns,
The voices of ancients stir the chains.
Each breeze carries tales of long-lost years,
Echoing softly, drowning our fears.

Mighty trees sway to an unknowable beat,
Guardians silent, their wisdom discreet.
Roots stretch deep into secrets profound,
While shadows dance, ghosts lost, but found.

The rustle of leaves, a soft-spoken prayer,
Inviting the dreamer, calling to dare.
What once was hidden, now flickers bright,
In the embrace of the warm, gentle night.

Where moonlight spills, and magic is spun,
Ancient spirits beckon, inviting the fun.
In the depths of the night, their stories partake,
Painting the world with each breath they make.

So linger a while, and heed their plea,
For the heart of the forest holds secrets to see.
In the canopy high, where silence reigns,
Voices of ancients whisper their chains.

The Quilted Night's Embrace

When stars unfold in a velvet sky,
The quilted night whispers a gentle sigh.
Each twinkling light tells stories untold,
Of dreams woven in silver and gold.

The moon hangs low, a guardian bright,
Guiding the lost through the cloak of night.
A tapestry woven of shadow and gleam,
Inviting the wanderer into the dream.

Soft breezes dance, weaving through trees,
Carrying notes of forgotten harmonies.
The night sings songs of love and desire,
Setting the soul and the heart afire.

In the quilted embrace, the world fades away,
And magic unfolds in a soft ballet.
With every heartbeat, a journey begins,
As stars shimmer quietly, the night softly spins.

So lie on the grass and gaze overhead,
Where dreams are born and whispers are fed.
In the warmth of the night, so tender and wise,
The quilted embrace brings peace to our eyes.

Veils of Mystery in Sundown Hues

In twilight's grasp, the shadows play,
Whispers dance on the edge of day.
Crimson skies with hints of gold,
Promises of secrets yet untold.

The trees stand tall, a guarding choir,
Crickets sing in the fading fire.
Denizens of dusk in veils entwined,
Their stories lost, yet intertwined.

A breeze stirs softly, a lover's sigh,
Carrying tales from the earth to sky.
As stars awaken in zephyr's embrace,
The night unfolds a hidden space.

With every step, the path reveals,
The magic stitched in nature's seals.
Lost in wonder, hearts align,
Under the spell of the twilight vine.

As shadows blend and colors fade,
In silence, nature's dream is laid.
Veils of mystery, bright and blue,
In sundown hues, our hopes renew.

Flickering Dreams among the Moss

In emerald depths, where the wildflowers sway,
Flickering dreams find a place to play.
Moss-covered stones cradle thoughts anew,
Whispers of wonders in shades of dew.

A gossamer thread weaves through the trees,
Carried by currents of forest breeze.
Each sigh of the land tells a story bright,
Bathed in the glow of the soft moonlight.

In shadowy corners where secrets lie,
Mirthful giggles of fairies fly.
Among the ferns and the ancient bark,
Little flickers ignite the dark.

As twilight dances on delicate shoes,
Flickering dreams are the heart's own muse.
Lost in a world where time stands still,
In that soft whisper, the heart can thrill.

Among the moss, where the wild things roam,
We find our peace, we find our home.
Each dream a lantern, guiding our way,
In the symphony of dusk, we wish to stay.

The Hidden Gems of Sylvan Serenity

Where streams reflect the glistening sun,
Hidden gems in the woodlands run.
Each petal holds a shimmering light,
Sylvan serenity, a true delight.

A tapestry woven of emerald green,
Every corner a wonder unseen.
The quiet song of the birds above,
Hums softly, a serenade of love.

Beneath the canopy, shadows play,
Glimmers of magic, come what may.
In nooks and crannies where creatures dwell,
Mysteries held in a woodland shell.

The hidden path, a corridor bold,
Leads to stories of ancients told.
With every footfall, the earth's sweet sigh,
Echoes gently, beneath the sky.

By peaceful brooks, where the wild things dream,
Flows the essence of nature's theme.
Hidden gems beneath the trees,
Gathering hearts in a whispered breeze.

Tales from the Moonlit Glade

In the moonlit glade, where shadows weave,
Tales are spun for those who believe.
A circle of stones, an ancient ring,
Hold the secrets of the night's sweet wing.

With every rustle, a legend lives,
Of whispered promises the forest gives.
Where creatures of magic infinitely roam,
The glade reveals its timeless home.

Underneath the stars, the world feels near,
Every heartbeat loud, echoing clear.
Night's tapestry, stitched with dreams,
Glows gently, unraveling seams.

Fables hidden in the twilight glow,
Carried on winds only the brave will know.
In the heart of the glade, wonders collide,
Binding us close, soft as the tide.

As dawn approaches with a silken sigh,
The tales linger, never truly die.
In the moonlit glade, where dreams are spun,
A promise remains with the rising sun.

Mysteries of the Gilded Canopy

Beneath the branches, shadows creep,
Whispers hold secrets, ancient and deep.
Golden sunlight filters through,
Dancing on leaves, a magical view.

Every flutter, every sigh,
Tales of the forest, hidden and spry.
Creatures roam in silken night,
Guardians of dreams, in whispered flight.

Curious eyes gaze wide and keen,
Finding the treasures, never seen.
Mysteries twine in nature's thread,
Stories untold, where few have tread.

Golden wings of fate take flight,
Stirring the magic, pure delight.
Underneath the gilded trees,
Hearts awaken with every breeze.

In the twilight, secrets wane,
Leaving echoes, like soft rain.
A canopy of dreams, so vast,
Where time stands still, shadowed and cast.

Shimmering Fragments in the Twilight

Twilight descends with colors aglow,
Shadows whisper secrets, soft and slow.
Stars begin to twinkle bright,
Illuminating the depths of night.

Petals glisten with dewdrop grace,
Each one a memory, time can't erase.
Fragments of laughter linger here,
As moonlight weaves its silver sphere.

Faint echoes shimmer, both near and far,
Guided by dreams, like a wishing star.
Each flame of light, a wish to find,
Bridges the gap of heart and mind.

In mossy glades, where secrets sleep,
Promises hidden, they quietly keep.
Tales of old in fragrant blooms,
Shattered candlelight in shadowed rooms.

With each sigh, the night unfurls,
Stories of magic, in sparkling swirls.
Fragments of dreams on twilight's crest,
Wrap the weary in comfort's rest.

The Elusive Spirit of the Thicket

In the thicket, shadows weave,
A spirit dances, none believe.
With laughter light, and eyes aglow,
It beckons forth those brave to go.

Veils of mist drape every tree,
Whispered tales of what might be.
Each rustling leaf, a sacred sound,
Where unseen wonders can be found.

Glimmers hidden in tangled wood,
Fables of old, understood.
A flicker here, a shimmer there,
The spirit's presence fills the air.

Beneath the boughs, where silence hums,
The thicket thrums with life that comes.
Elusive journeys, wondrous and free,
Whispers that dance in twilight's plea.

So venture deep, if you dare,
To find the spirit, elusive and rare.
In every heartbeat, a secret lies,
Woven in nature, under the skies.

Shades of Enchantment in Leafy Realms

In leafy realms, enchantment sings,
Where every branch a story brings.
Colors blend in nature's art,
Whispers of magic, heart to heart.

Moss carpets the earth, soft and green,
A tapestry of dreams, serene.
Light filters down, a golden glow,
Hiding the treasures only few know.

Amidst the ferns, shadows play,
In gentle winds, they weave and sway.
An ancient wisdom, rich and pure,
In every leaf, it seeks to lure.

Flickering lights, fireflies dance,
In the quiet night, casting a glance.
The realms of wonder, vast and wide,
Where hope and joy gently reside.

So wander deep, in twilight's embrace,
To find the enchantment of this place.
In shades of green, your spirit may roam,
Finding enchantment, forever home.

Secrets of the Weeping Willows

Beneath the boughs where shadows dwell,
The whispers weave a silent spell.
With every rustle, secrets sigh,
In twilight's breath, they float and fly.

The ancient roots hold tales untold,
Of lovers lost and dreams of gold.
The bark, a canvas, rough yet wise,
Hides mysteries beneath the skies.

In moonbeam's glow, the stories dance,
Inviting hearts to take a chance.
With every droop and gentle sway,
They beckon souls to wade and play.

The weeping willows veil the night,
Embracing all in soft twilight.
Where secrets linger, softly spun,
And echoes fade with setting sun.

So step with care, dear wanderer,
Within this realm of creepers' blur.
For in their shade, the heart may find,
A world where magic gently binds.

Sparks of Magic through the Thorns

Amidst the brambles, fierce and wild,
A melody sweet, yet softly riled.
The thorns may prick, yet beauty glows,
With sparks of magic that none but knows.

Each thorn, a guardian, holds the light,
Guiding lost souls through the night.
With every step, the heart must trust,
In shadows deep, there's wonder's dust.

Through twisted paths, the secrets blend,
As fleeting moments twist and bend.
Like fireflies trapped in velvet air,
Each spark unveiled, a whispered prayer.

The thorns may cut, yet love will bloom,
In darkest corners, dispelling gloom.
Where pain meets joy in daring flight,
Amidst the brambles, hearts ignite.

So gather 'round, and do not fear,
The magic flows, the path is clear.
With courage borne from every thorn,
New wonders greet the newly born.

The Lullaby of the Sylvan Dusk

Beneath the trees where shadows creep,
A lullaby whispers, soft and deep.
The dusk descends, in hues of blue,
A magic cradle, old yet new.

Each leaf sings low in gentle tones,
And as night falls, the heart atones.
With breezes curling soft like dreams,
In sylvan realms, all is not as it seems.

The brook hums sweet, a tranquil guide,
While starlit skies unfold wide.
Embrace the dusk; let silence reign,
For here, the lost find love again.

In twilight's hush, all fears take flight,
As moonlight weaves through hands of night.
A spectral dance of shadows near,
The lullaby, a soothing cheer.

So close your eyes, dear dreamer bold,
In sylvan dusk, the tales are told.
With every note, let hopes unfurl,
In nature's arms, a wondrous whirl.

Puddles of Light in the Enchanted Wild

In woodland's heart, where wonders gleam,
Lie puddles of light, a sparkling dream.
Reflecting stars from realms above,
In every ripple, magic's love.

The ferns stand tall, like sentinels,
Guarding secrets that nature tells.
Each glimmer dances, inviting near,
In enchanted wild, there's naught to fear.

With every step, new treasures found,
As gentle whispers pulse the ground.
The air is thick with stories spun,
Amidst the hues of setting sun.

So leap through light, where shadows play,
With laughter singing, chase away.
The puddles beckon, soft and bright,
In their embrace, all feels just right.

In nature's arms, take heart and tread,
Where wild things dance, and fears are shed.
For in the wild, the soul takes flight,
In puddles of joy, pure delight.

The Secret Life of the Moonlit Glade

In the hush of night's embrace,
Shadows dance with gentle grace.
Stars peek through the leafy seam,
Whispers weave a silver dream.

Owls call softly, secrets sigh,
Creatures hidden, they watch nearby.
Moonbeams drape the forest's gown,
Magic stirs where none are found.

A brook glimmers, a silken thread,
Carrying stories, long since said.
Luminous tales in ripples spun,
Echoing softly till night's undone.

Beneath the boughs, where shadows loom,
Hearts awaken to nature's tune.
In the moonlit glade's embrace,
Wonder thrives in sacred space.

Time drifts slowly, moments blend,
Lost in magic, we transcend.
Every sigh and every glance,
Lives entwined in a twilight dance.

Threads of Silver among the Bark

Silver threads in twilight's weave,
Traced through time, a gift to leave.
Nestled close in tree's embrace,
Nature's wisdom knows no space.

Each gnarled branch and tender leaf,
Hides whispers of both joy and grief.
The forest's breath, a gentle sigh,
Tales of ages passing by.

Sunlight filters, a painted glow,
Guiding hearts where wildthings grow.
With every step, the past unfolds,
In the roots, a secret holds.

The bark remembers, every scar,
Stories etched, both near and far.
Threads of silver, memories bound,
In the quiet, solace found.

Nature's tapestry, rich and bright,
Weaving dreams in soft moonlight.
A journey through the ages' thread,
Where all who wander gently tread.

The Enigma of the Verdant Whisper

In morning's glow, the forest sighs,
A verdant whisper, soft replies.
Leaves unfurl on gentle breeze,
Telling tales of hidden keys.

Mossy carpets, emerald deep,
Secrets in the shadows creep.
A melody of life awakens,
In every breath, the wild is taken.

Sunbeams dance through kin to kin,
Nature beckons, draw us in.
With every step, the mystery grows,
In verdant realms where magic flows.

Curiosity stirs the mind,
With every whisper, truth we find.
The forest holds, in leafy throng,
An enigma sung in nature's song.

Embrace the hush, the sacred space,
Where heartbeats meet in nature's grace.
In verdant whispers, dreams take flight,
Bringing light to the forest's night.

Petals Adrift in Sunset's Breath

Petals drift where sunbeams fall,
Carried softly by twilight's call.
A fragrant dance, in golden hue,
Whispers of dusk, a world anew.

Crimson skies and lavender trails,
Each petal holds a story's scales.
Breezes whisper of love once born,
As twilight casts its gentle morn.

Golden horizons wrap the day,
In dreams of blooms that gently sway.
Fleeting moments, captured grace,
Time stands still in nature's embrace.

Falling softly, the petals weave,
A tapestry the heart believes.
In every drift, a memory stays,
In sunset's breath, love softly plays.

As night descends, the petals rest,
In slumber's fold, they're ever blessed.
In the hush of twilight's gleam,
Life awakens in each dream.

Whispers of Enchanted Fragments

In the woods where shadows play,
A soft breeze carries dreams away.
Fragments glint like stars on high,
Whispers float beneath the sky.

Crickets sing their lullabies,
Echoing through night's disguise.
Each rustle tells a tale untold,
Of secret worlds where magic's bold.

Mossy stones where fairies tread,
Glowing softly, visions spread.
Glimmers dance on silver streams,
Life unfolds in quiet dreams.

Old oaks bear the scars of time,
Holding secrets, steeped in rhyme.
Roots entwine like whispered vows,
Nature's heart, it gently bows.

A soft fog wraps the grove tight,
Wrapped in mystery, shrouded light.
With each turn, the path does twist,
In this world, none can resist.

So linger long where wonders bloom,
Let daylight melt into the gloom.
For in these woods, lost dreams awake,
In whispered tones, the heart shall quake.

Glimmers of Woodland Secrets

Through the trees, the sunlight breaks,
Lighting paths that nature makes.
Whispers dance upon the breeze,
Glimmers flicker through the leaves.

Mushrooms glow in twilight's grace,
In this still and sacred place.
Each flower opens, secrets share,
In the cool, enchanted air.

Rabbits dart where shadows creep,
While ancient oaks their secrets keep.
Where laughter mingles with the sighs,
Of whispers lost 'neath starlit skies.

The brook hums songs of ages past,
Carving dreams that forever last.
Ripples mirror whispers' play,
In twilight's soft, embracing sway.

Beckoning with every sound,
Nature's heart beats all around.
In every glance, a tale awaits,
In woodland realms where wonder waits.

So follow where the path does weave,
In magic's dance, you shall believe.
For in this world of secrets deep,
The heart finds joy, the spirit leaps.

Beneath the Canopy's Embrace

In the hush of morning's glow,
Whispers linger, soft and slow.
Beneath the leaves, the stories swirl,
Each petal holds a hidden pearl.

Sunlight dapples mossy ground,
In this haven, peace is found.
Nature sings a serene refrain,
As shadows dance like gentle rain.

A faun's laugh, a nymph's sweet song,
Here, in realms where you belong.
With breathless awe, you take your stand,
In this enchanted, fairytale land.

Twisted roots and ancient stone,
Guarding secrets set in bone.
Branches sway, the breeze does tease,
With stories carried on the breeze.

As daylight fades, the stars ignite,
Filling the woods with silver light.
Beneath the canopy's embrace,
You find a moment, time's sweet grace.

So linger here, let worries cease,
In nature's arms, you feel the peace.
For when you wander through this place,
You find your heart in magic's grace.

Fragments of Twilight's Dance

In twilight's glow, the world transforms,
As shadows whirl in graceful swarms.
The sky blushes in hues of gold,
While dusk unveils the dreams of old.

Glimmers spark in fading light,
Nature hums a soft delight.
Whispers weave through air so sweet,
As day and night in wonder meet.

The brook reflects a starry veil,
Carrying tales of nightingale.
In silence, secrets weave their threads,
As twilight dances on soft beds.

Owls awaken, their wisdom flows,
Through tranquil nights where magic grows.
With every note, the forest sings,
Of hidden dreams and wondrous things.

Softly now the night descends,
Where muffled laughter never ends.
In cozy nooks, the heart expands,
To join the rhythm of nature's hands.

So breathe it in, this fleeting trance,
As stars arise to join the dance.
For in the twilight's tender glance,
We find our place in magic's chance.

Dance of the Sylvan Reflections

In whispers soft, the forest breathes,
Beneath the boughs where magic weaves.
The silver stars in twilight gleam,
While shadows move like a waking dream.

With every step, the flowers sway,
As if to join in the night's ballet.
The crickets chirp a gentle tune,
While echoes waltz beneath the moon.

A flicker here, a glint of light,
The sylphs assemble, shy from sight.
They twirl and spin in gossamer grace,
A surreal dance in this enchanted place.

The brook hums low; the air is sweet,
With scents of thyme and moss beneath.
In glades adorned with twilight's lace,
The sylvan spirits find their place.

And as the night begins to fade,
The dance will still, yet never jade.
For in the heart of every glen,
The magic lingers, time and again.

Mysteries of the Amber Meadow

Upon the hill, where daisies play,
The sun casts gold on bright bouquet.
In every petal, secrets lie,
Of whispered dreams that drift on high.

The rustling grass tells tales of yore,
Of fleeting souls who danced before.
They left their laughter on the breeze,
In amber hues among the trees.

Here, time is woven with delight,
As shadows mingle with the light.
A beckoning path calls you to roam,
In search of wonders yet unknown.

The butterflies weave a tapestry,
Of colors bright, like poetry.
Each flutter holds a story told,
In dreams of silver, hints of gold.

So linger long in this embrace,
Where nature cradles every grace.
In amber's glow, the mysteries flow,
A meadow's heart, forever aglow.

Shadows of the Emerald Veil

In glades where emerald shadows reign,
The whispered secrets fall like rain.
A world of wonder waits to be found,
Where fairies gather on hallowed ground.

The ancient trees in quiet prayer,
Stand sentinel in the woodland air.
Their branches arch, a leafy dome,
Embracing all who wander home.

The silver mist begins to rise,
As twilight paints the darkening skies.
With every breath, the magic grows,
In hidden realms where no one knows.

The shadows dance beneath the light,
With flickering forms of pure delight.
They weave a spell, both soft and grand,
In the emerald clasp of this land.

So tread with care, and listen well,
To the stories only the shadows tell.
For in each whisper of the night,
Lies the promise of soft twilight.

Fractured Light in the Fairy Realm

In twilight's grip, the echoes play,
As beams of light begin to stray.
With every shimmer, dreams collide,
In the fairy realm where hopes abide.

The lanterns glow with magic bright,
Inviting wanderers to dance in flight.
Through fields of twinkling, fleeting spark,
The fairies flit within the dark.

With laughter sweet, like crystal chimes,
They weave their tales in waltzing rhymes.
Each burst of color, a canvas bold,
Of fractured light, their stories told.

The brook reflects their playful sighs,
As stardust drifts through velvet skies.
Each flicker brims with life anew,
In this enchanted realm, where dreams come true.

So press your ear to the night's allure,
For magic lingers, bright and pure.
In the fractured light, take your chance,
And join the fairies in their dance.

The Enchanted Symphony of Twilight

In twilight's arms, the whispers play,
Notes of magic float away.
A melody fraught with hidden dreams,
Echoes of time in silver beams.

The starry skies begin to glow,
As shadows dance beneath the bow.
With each chord, the night unfolds,
A tale of wonder softly told.

Gentle winds caress the air,
While moonlit whispers lay us bare.
In harmony, the world takes flight,
A symphony of pure delight.

Each shimmer a secret, each flicker a rhyme,
As twilight twirls, suspending time.
Lost in the music, hearts entwined,
In an enchanted world, love is defined.

So let the symphony carry you high,
On wings of dreams through the sapphire sky.
For in this moment, magical and free,
The twilight's song binds you and me.

Secrets Swirling in the Autumn Breeze

Leaves tumble down, a crisp ballet,
Carried by whispers of a fading day.
Each swirl reveals a mystery spun,
Beneath the autumn's setting sun.

Golden hues paint the cool, brisk air,
While secrets linger, everywhere.
In the rustling groves, stories unfold,
Of ancient times and treasures bold.

Branches sway with a knowing sigh,
As shadows creep, and memories lie.
In the dance of dusk, what tales reside?
A tapestry woven where dreams abide.

The world feels hushed, wrapped in a cloak,
As the breeze shares the words it spoke.
From tree to tree, the secrets weave,
In the heart of fall, we dare to believe.

So gather 'round as the daylight wanes,
Embrace the magic that autumn gains.
In the swirling leaves, let your heart soar,
For in each whisper, there's so much more.

Lanterns of Sorrow in Forest Depths

Deep in the woods where shadows dwell,
Lanterns flicker with tales to tell.
Each light a tear, a tranquil sigh,
Guiding lost souls who wander by.

Gnarled branches reach for the starry skies,
As whispers echo and softly rise.
In the silence, a haunting grace,
Illuminates every hidden space.

Time stands still in the forest's embrace,
Each lantern a memory, a clouded face.
With every flicker, the past ignites,
A dance of sorrow in endless nights.

Yet through the gloom, there's hope anew,
As lanterns gleam with a tender hue.
Though heartache lingers in shadowed glen,
There's light beyond the dark again.

So walk with courage, and don't despair,
For in the depths, love lingers there.
Let the lanterns guide your path so true,
Through sorrow's veil, to skies of blue.

The Elfin Star's Tender Dance

In the hush of night, the starry sprite,
Weaves through dreams, a shimmering light.
With gentle grace, it spirals and twirls,
Painting the sky with sparkles and pearls.

A dance of joy, so soft, so free,
In the moon's warm glow, beneath the tree.
Elfin whispers in the chilling air,
Caress the heart with a timeless care.

Among the blooms of nocturnal delight,
Where shadows play and hearts take flight.
Each leap and bound, a tale to share,
Echoes of laughter entwined with prayer.

In twilight's embrace, the magic unfolds,
With every shimmer, a story told.
As starlight sings its tender refrain,
Love dances softly through joy and pain.

So gaze upon the sky so vast,
With hope anew, let your dreams be cast.
For in the dance of the elfin star,
You'll find the way, no matter how far.

Love Letters from the Gloomy Wood

In shadows deep where secrets dwell,
The trees compose a darkened spell.
Their whispers weave a tender thread,
Each leaf a word, each sigh unsaid.

Kissed by the moon's soft silver light,
The heartache dances near the night.
With every rustle, hope takes flight,
In gloomy woods, love's pure delight.

Through tangled boughs, our dreams take shape,
A fragile bond, a whispered tape.
In every pause, a promise lies,
Beneath the watchful, starlit skies.

The plucking strings of nightbird's song,
In lonely realms, where we belong.
A symphony of sweet despair,
In gloomy woods, love lingers there.

As twilight falls, the world creates,
A canvas where our fate awaits.
In every glance, a fleeting glance,
Our shadows meet in silent dance.

Echoes of the Emerald Whisper

Amidst the leaves, where green dreams bloom,
Echoes stir in nature's room.
A gentle breeze sings soft and low,
Carrying tales only few can know.

In every glance, the forest sighs,
With secrets wrapped in emerald ties.
The sunlight weaves through branches tight,
Painting shadows, igniting night.

Beneath the boughs, where laughter dwells,
Memories linger, time repells.
Each note a gem, a timeless grace,
Echoes whisper in nature's embrace.

The fables spun from vibrant hues,
In spiraled knots of varying clues.
A melody born from ancient streams,
Echoes hum of forgotten dreams.

So close your eyes and feel the lore,
The emerald whispers, forevermore.
Embrace the sounds, let them be found,
In echoes soft, where love is crowned.

Notes from the Celestial Canopy

Beneath the stars, the heavens hum,
In cosmic waves, our hearts succumb.
The night unveils its vast array,
Notes of joy in night's ballet.

Each twinkling light, a whispered call,
Inviting dreams to rise or fall.
The moon's soft glow, a guiding hand,
A serenade from a silver band.

In silent realms, where wishes soar,
The cosmic dance reveals much more.
With every star, a chance to seek,
The universe speaks, gentle and meek.

Through constellations, stories thread,
Of love long lost, and tears we shed.
Each note a wish, each sigh a tale,
In celestial dance, we shall prevail.

So lift your gaze, embrace the night,
And let your heart take flight, take flight.
For in the notes that softly sway,
Lies the promise of another day.

The Gentle Murmurs of the Night

When twilight falls, the world transforms,
With gentle murmurs, the night conforms.
The hush of stars, a soothing balm,
In darkened hours, a vibrant calm.

Each whisper travels on the breeze,
Carrying hopes like autumn leaves.
The moonlight dances on the stream,
Sketching shadows, igniting dreams.

With every sigh, the night reveals,
The tender truths that silence feels.
In hushed tones, the world unfolds,
A tapestry of stories told.

The distant call of nightingale,
Echoes softly, soothing scale.
The gentle murmurs blend and flow,
In twilight's grasp, love's seeds we sow.

So linger here, where hearts unite,
In the gentle murmurs of the night.
Let time stand still, let worries cease,
In whispered dreams, we find our peace.

www.ingramcontent.com/pod-product-compliance
Ingram Content Group UK Ltd.
Pitfield, Milton Keynes, MK11 3LW, UK
UKHW021417230125
4262UKWH00028B/351